Discover and Share

Animal Homes

Deborah Chancellor

W

FRANKLIN WATTS

LONDON•SYDNEY

About this book

The **Discover and Share** series enables young readers to read about familiar topics independently. The books are designed to build on children's existing knowledge while providing new information and vocabulary. By sharing this book, either with an adult or another child, young children can learn how to access information, build word recognition skills and develop reading confidence in an enjoyable way.

Reading tips

- Begin by finding out what children already know about the topic. Encourage them to talk about it and take the opportunity to introduce vocabulary specific to the topic.

- Each image is explained through two levels of text. Confident readers will be able to read the higher level text independently, while emerging readers can try reading the simpler sentences.

- Check for understanding of any unfamiliar words and concepts. Inexperienced readers might need you to read some or all of the text to them. Encourage children to retell the information in their own words.

- After you have explored the book together, try the quiz on page 22 to see what children can remember and to encourage further discussion.

Contents

Words in **bold** are in the glossary on page 23.

Safe shelter

You need somewhere to rest and keep warm. It is the same for animals. All living things need a safe place to **shelter**.

Animals make their homes in different places. Some live high up in trees. Others live under the ground.

You need a safe place to rest.
It is the same for animals!

Snowy home

This polar bear is hard to spot in the snow. Her cubs are born in a den.

The polar bear lives in the Arctic, where it is freezing cold. The bear's thick fur keeps it warm and **camouflaged** in the snow.

In winter, the female polar bear digs a snowy den. It is cosy here for her cubs.

Underground town

These prairie dogs live in burrows. The burrows are under the ground.

Prairie dogs live in the **plains** of North America. They dig deep under the ground to make a hidden maze of burrows.

A set of prairie dog burrows is called a town. Just one town can be the size of a football pitch!

Tall tower

Tiny insects called termites live together in a group called a **colony**. Different termites do different jobs. For example, workers find food and soldiers **defend** the colony.

Most termites live in nests under the ground, but some build very tall towers.

Termites live in a nest. Some termite nests are very tall.

11

Dark cave

The fruit bat flies around at night, looking for fruit and **nectar** to eat. Fruit bats **roost** together in dark caves. They hang upside-down, gripping onto the rock with their sharp claws.

Bats look for food at night.
They sleep in dark caves in the day.

Rocky rest

A golden eagle's nest is high in a tree or on a cliff. It is called an **eyrie**. The nest is made of branches.

This golden eagle's nest is on a rocky cliff.

15

Grassy nest

The harvest mouse spends most of the year underground. It lives in burrows made by other animals.

In summer, a female harvest mouse builds a nest in tall grasses. She has two or three **litters** of baby mice in her nest.

In summer, this harvest mouse makes a nest. Her babies are born in the nest.

17

Hermit home

Hermit crabs don't have a hard shell of their own, so they borrow one to protect themselves from **predators.** They live in empty sea shells.

Hermit crabs can grow up to ten centimetres long. When they get too big for their shell, they find a new one.

Hermit crabs live in shells.
The shell keeps the crab safe.

Fishy shelter

Clown fish shelter in **anemones**, which are a kind of sea animal. They are the only fish that are not hurt by an anemone's sting.

Clown fish and anemones help each other. Clown fish eat the scraps that fall on anemones. They need food, and anemones need to keep clean.

Clown fish shelter in this anemone.
The fish keep the anemone clean. 21

Quiz

1. Why do polar bears have thick fur?

2. What is a prairie dog town?

3. What lives in this tall tower?

4. Where do fruit bats sleep?

Glossary

anemones sea animals that look like plants

camouflaged blending in with the background

colony a group of animals that live together

defend to keep safe

eyrie an eagle's nest

litters sets of babies born at the same time

nectar the sweet liquid found in flowers

plains flat land covered in grass

predators animals that hunt other animals

roost to settle down to rest or sleep

shelter to find protection from weather or danger

Answers to quiz: 1. It helps them to keep warm. 2. A set of burrows. 3. Termites live there. 4. They sleep in caves.

Index

First published in 2013 by
Franklin Watts
338 Euston Road
London
NW1 3BH

Franklin Watts Australia
Level 17/207 Kent Street
Sydney
NSW 2000

Copyright © Franklin Watts 2013

HB ISBN 978 1 4451 1732 4
Library ebook ISBN 978 1 4451 2496 4

Dewey number: 591.5'64
A CIP catalogue record for this book is
available from the British Library.

Series Editor: Julia Bird
Series Advisor: Karina Law
Series Design: Basement68

Picture credits: Michal Bednarak/Dreamstime: 4. bluehand/
Shutterstock: 3b, 20. Roger de la Harpe/Corbis: 13, 22br. Eric Isselee/
Shutterstock: 1,18. Hugh Landsdown/Shutterstock: 12. Janelle Lugge/
Shutterstock: 11, 22bl. Mark Malkinson/Alamy: 16. Kelvin Marshall/PD:
10. David McKee/Shutterstock: 21. Roberta Olenick/Getty Images: 15.
Myroslav Orshak/Shutterstock: front cover, 19. Jenny E Ross/Corbis: 7.
Susanne Sanders/Foto Natura/Corbis: 8, 22cr. Scott Tilley/Alamy: 5.
David Tipling/Alamy: 17. Tom Vezo/Minden Pictures/FLPA: 3t, 14.
Wild Arctic Pictures/Shutterstock: 6, 22cl. Shin Yoshino/Corbis: 9.

Printed in China

Franklin Watts is a division of
Hachette Children's Books,
an Hachette UK company.
www.hachette.co.uk